Harold the Hippo & Drucilla Duck at Poundly Pond

BOOK II

Written by
David Underhill

Based on an idea by
Samantha Underhill

INTRODUCTION

This is the beginning of some stories of friendship between the characters who lived around a beautiful village called Poundly Pond where some of the grass had been eaten and some was quite long and lush.

They even include a number of events that took place between some of those who lived in a couple of nearby villages; some just came to visit and play games whilst some even played in the pond.

I hope you enjoy these friendly stories and even personalise them with your own colours to make them look how you want them to.

DEDICATION PAGE

This book of stories about 'Harold and Drucilla at Poundly Pond' is dedicated to my grandchildren : Lucas, Logan and Oliver, as they slowly get older, read them and even colour them for themselves. It is also dedicated to all children who read the stories and want to colour them whilst they create their own stories.

Harold the Hippo & Drucilla Duck at Poundly Pond Book II

Written by
David J V Underhill.
63 Dacombe Drive.
Upton. Poole. BH16 5JJ

Based on an idea by
Samantha Underhill.

THE CAMPING TRIP

It had been in the depth of a very cold winter that Harold, Drucilla, Robert and Georgina had decided that they were going to have a camping holiday, but they did not know where they were going until there was only two weeks before they were due to go. They decided to go to the Lake District. None of them had ever been to the Lake District before. None of them had even been camping before either but they decided that no matter what happened they would have a great time.

So that they did not have to carry too much they arranged to hire the tents from a shop in a town close to where they were going, they would also hire all the other equipment they would need like a stove, plates, cups, knives & forks and a special light that ran on paraffin called a tilley lamp.

The friends all went shopping during the last week to buy the things they thought that they would need. They each bought a rucksack, a sleeping bag, some warm clothes, waterproofs and warm waterproof boots. When they arrived home they had a fashion parade. How they all laughed at each other as they paraded in their bright yellow or orange waterproof suits and their walking boots.

Two days before they were due to leave all the friends got together to check that they had everything ready. They checked off their things from a list that they had all agreed would be needed - warm clothes like jumpers, trousers, shirts and vests, lots of socks, pants. Then other things like washing gear, towels, pyjamas, swimming costumes and spare shoes. They each had to take a torch and spare batteries, they took one radio between them and a selection of books to read. If there was any space left they then squeezed in anything else, they wanted. The sleeping bags were then strapped on the top of each rucksack and the walking boots were tied around the straps. They would not need them until they had collected the camping gear and were making their way out into the countryside.

The day to start their holiday had finally arrived, it was Friday 23rd June and although it was only six o'clock in the morning inside four houses in Poundly Pond there were alarm clocks chiming and four sleepy people waking from a good night's sleep. Each of them got dressed and had a good breakfast, they did not know exactly when they were going to eat again, it may not be for several hours. Outside it was dry and already the sun was shining brightly, it looked as though it was going to be a good day. They had decided to meet at Georgina's house at a quarter to seven, they chose Georgina's because it was closest to the bus stop and the others would have to go past it anyway. Sure enough at seventeen minutes to seven, two minutes early, they were all ready to go. After a last check that they had everything they started walking up the road to catch the seven o'clock bus.

The bus arrived on time and slowed to a stop, the door opened and the four friends climbed up into the bus. As the driver saw them he was surprised at the big rucksacks on their backs.
"Going on holiday?" he asked.
"Yes" they all answered together " to the Lake District"
They all paid their fare and each found a seat. There were only two other people on the bus so they had plenty of seats to choose from, they each sat on one seat, two on each side of the isle.

After about twenty minutes the bus came to the train station and they all got off. "Have a good time" said the driver.
"Thank you" they all said in reply as they pulled on the rucksacks.

They made their way to the ticket office and one by one they bought their tickets. "One return to Windermere please" they all said. "£10-60 please" was the answer each time as the ticket shot out of the machine in front of them. Having found out which platform the train was due to leave from and checked that it was on time they decided to have a cup of tea. They had about twenty minutes to wait so there was time for a short rest. They had talked about the holiday for weeks but they still found things to talk about, they were clearly looking forward to their adventure.

With a whistle the train pulled slowly into the station and as it reached the signal at end it let out a hiss as it finally stopped. The platform was a hive of activity, several doors had opened and out stepped people on their way to work. Other people standing on the platform stepped up into the carriages, there were people in smart suits, there were children in school uniform, there were several families with suitcases and there was a trolley piled high with mail sacks that was being unloaded. Finally, at two minutes to eight with a whistle and a hiss of steam the train started again. Slowly the train went at first, gradually it went faster until they were out into the countryside and all they could hear was the clickety click clickety click of the wheels on the rails, every now and again they heard the trains whistle and a roar as they went through a tunnel or under a bridge. Occasionally they would stop at stations on the way where some people got off and others got on.

The train journey would take about five hours so they all started reading or looking out of the window at the fields and towns that passed by. They also played a few games like snap and draughts. Robert even went to sleep.
As the time approached one o'clock and they neared their

destination the train started to slow down, Robert had woken up and they all started putting away the books and other things that they had been doing. They also decided to put their walking boots on. It was seven minutes past one o'clock as the train pulled in at Windermere station, as it bumped to a stop Harold opened the carriage door and one by one they got out, several other people also got off the train and some got on. They walked along the platform as the train pulled away again with a whistle and a hiss. They showed their tickets to the guard who clipped them to indicate that they had been checked, they then walked out of the station and down the hill towards the town where they would pick up the tents and other equipment.

By now they were beginning to feel quite hungry so after finding the hire shop and collecting everything they found a cafe where they stopped for something to eat and drink.

After about half an hour they decided that they ought to start walking to the camp site, after all it would take about two hours to get there. They left the town and started up the first hill, after only twenty minutes they could not see the town any more as it was behind the hill. All they could see were more hills, heather, trees, a few sheep, the road and a lake in the distance. Happily, they walked along the road until they came to a fork where they went right, the road gradually dipped downwards towards to lake that they had seen in the distance. They had not seen any cars or other people since they had left the town but there in front of them, in the middle of nowhere, was a place that they could rest and have something to eat and drink if they wanted to, it was called 'The Greystoke'. Outside were two cars, a motorbike and several bicycles. Three people were sitting round a table in the garden and two children were playing on the grass.

They all sat at another table whilst Harold went inside to get them all a drink, minutes later he came back with four tall glasses full of ice and home-made lemonade. They all agreed that it tasted wonderful. Whilst inside Harold had asked directions to the camp site because he thought it was quite close, the landlord had confirmed that the turning was only another two miles down the road and the site was then just under one mile up the path. They thought that it would take them about an hour to get there so, reluctantly they left the table and having said good-bye they set off again.

By now they were getting rather tired and it seemed to have been such a long time since they last sat down, at last they saw the turning to the right. The sign post said Little Windem Camp Site. With a renewed bounce in their step they almost started running, but after several steps they slowed down again and just walked quickly. Upon turning yet another bend they saw the main gate to the camp site, beyond it was the office and beyond that was the field where they would put their tents.

The door of the office opened and out stepped an Otter, " Mr Livingstone I presume" he said with a laugh "Welcome to my camp site" just then Mrs Otter appeared with a tray on which were four glasses of orange juice.

"I thought you might like a drink" said Mrs Otter "after all it has been rather hot today"

"Thank you" they all said together setting down their rucksacks and tents and taking a glass, " It has been hot today, especially carrying this lot" said Drucilla pointing to her pile.

Whilst they drank their orange, Harold had arranged with Mr Otter where the best place for them to put their tents would be, he also paid for the use of the site. It was £1 per person per week, so as they were staying for two weeks that was £8. Mr Otter also showed Harold where the toilets and showers were.

"Come on" said Harold we had better start putting up the tents and get ourselves settled. So having thanked Mrs Otter again they put on the rucksacks and picked up the tents and other items, then they walked across the field and over a small stream. "That's the shower block" said Harold as they passed a white building. They reached a small copse that nearly surrounded a clearing. "Mr Otter said that this was the best place for us to set up" said Harold, so with a sigh of relief they put down everything.

As Drucilla put her things down she turned and looked through the gap on the far side of the clearing, she went to say something but stopped, her mouth was open in stunned silence. "Look at the view" she stammered. They all turned and looked. They could see for miles along a valley, there were hills on each side and a lake in the bottom that seemed to stretch forever. "It's beautiful" said Georgina. "Yes" said Harold calmly "Mr Otter said that this was the best place to see the view."

"It certainly is" said Drucilla, now that she had got her voice back "It certainly is".

It took them more than half an hour of laughter to put the tents up, then another half an hour of more laughter to get their beds ready and sort out all the equipment. Another hour was spent having something to eat and clear up, after which they were all so tired that they decided to go to bed. Two at a time they went to the shower block, and as each of them crawled into bed they were instantly asleep.

As the sun rose the next morning it revealed the view that they had seen the night before, only now there were shafts of light shining down the valley and on to the lake making it sparkle. None of them had ever seen anything like it, they decided to walk down to the lake and have a swim. Having clambered down the hill, climbed over a stile and walked along a path a little way they finally came to the edge of the lake. From here the view was still spectacular and the lake looked even bigger.
They had a wonderful swim although the water was a little cold, during the next two weeks they spent quite a lot of time by the lake.

There were several places to visit so they spent two weeks swimming, walking, exploring and sitting in the sun. They visited 'The Greystoke' where they had the home-made lemonade, they even found several ruins in the hills. Each night they returned to the tents quite exhausted and after a good meal they slept soundly until the next morning. On the last night they had been invited to dinner at the house with Mr & Mrs Otter where they had a wonderful feast of stuffed tomatoes and marrow's, with lots of potato, carrots, peas and corn on the cob. After the meal they all thanked Mrs Otter for a wonderful meal and they said that they did not really want to leave. They promised to come back to Little

Windem again, they all said good night and went back to their tents.

The next day Mr Otter offered to take their tents and rucksacks into town for them so that they could spend the last morning swimming in the lake. Down to the lake they went and splashed around for two hours but unfortunately it was finally time to leave, so they dressed and began the walk back to the town where they would catch the train back home. As they passed the house they said good-bye to Mrs Otter, then they said good-bye to the landlord at the Greystoke who waved to them as they walked past. Because they were not carrying anything heavy it only took them just under one and a half hours to reach the town. They met Mr Otter outside the hire shop and thanked him for taking their things in his truck. After returning the equipment to the shop they walked up the hill to the station, they did not have to wait more than ten minutes before the train came round the bend and stopped at the station.

The friends were quite sad as the train pulled out of the station, they looked back over the town towards the camp site but it was beyond the next hill so they could not see it. They settled down and all they could hear was the clickety click clickety click of the wheels on the rails, the roar as they went through a tunnel or under a bridge and the whistle of the train as it approached each station. The time seemed to pass so quickly and the next thing they knew was that the train was pulling into the station where they had to get off. After making sure that they had left nothing behind they all got off the train and stood watching it pull away again with a whistle and a hiss.

It was now almost five o'clock, just in time to catch the last bus back to Poundly Pond. "Hello" said the driver as they got on the bus. "Did you have a good time?"
"Yes thank you" they replied " we didn't really want to come back".

Twenty minutes later they were getting off the bus and walking back down the road. " Oh well" said Robert "I suppose it had to end sometime, we couldn't stay there forever"
"No" said Georgina " We couldn't could we"
They continued talking all the way down the road until they reached Georgina's house where they went their separate ways. "Good bye" they all said. "Good bye".

THE TRIP TO FRANCE

Drucilla had always wanted to see other places and visit other countries and although Harold told her all about the places he had been it was not the same as seeing it for herself.

Without Drucilla knowing Harold had made enquiries about places they could go, he had also asked some of their friends if they too would like to go on a trip. But he made them promise not to tell Drucilla as it was to be a surprise.

Charlene and Ricky decided to go, and eventually they agreed with

Harold that they should go to France, after all it was not too far to Southampton where they could catch a ferry. Only Harold had been across the sea before so the others did not know what to expect.

Harold booked the tickets and then with only 1 week to go he told Drucilla. She was so surprised that she flew into a panic but quickly she calmed down and hugged Harold, thanking him very much. The next few days were spent packing suitcases and making sure that they had everything ready.

Finally, the day came for them to go and although they were only going for four days they had nine suitcases between them as well as several small bags. Harold and Ricky had three suitcases each, Charlene had two and Drucilla had one big one.
They did look funny walking up the road to the bus stop, but after several of the cases were dropped, Ricky falling over his own feet and even Harold forgetting his camera they reached the end of the road and stood waiting for the bus.

It had been a lovely walk up the road because, being spring time, all the trees and flowers were in full bloom and the air had a wonderful fresh smell. All around the bus stop was so pretty, even the farmers' fields were in colour. After a little wait the bus arrived and the pals all got on. Fortunately, there were not many others on the bus because the suitcases took up a lot of room.

After about an hour they reached the bus dept in Southampton from where they only had to walk a short distance to the ferry. Having travelled before Harold was quite calm but the others were obviously excited and they walked very quickly although they had plenty of time.

When they reached the ferry they had to go up the gang plank, this was not easy for the Harold or Ricky with their three suitcases, even Drucilla struggled with her one large one. Eventually they were all on board and seated in the front lounge with their cases safely stacked in the luggage area.

The sun was shining and there was a slight warm breeze, it was a glorious day and as they sat there looking out over the sea, watching the birds swoop and soar overhead, the ferry jerked into life as it slowly pulled away from the quay. It would take about three hours to reach France so there was plenty of time to explore.

There was the tea room where sandwiches and lovely sticky buns could be eaten with a drink of tea, orange, coffee or even just water. They could walk all around the ferry, they could see where they had come from and where they were going. They could sit out on the deck taking in the sun or they could sit in the comfort of the lounge. With all these things to do the journey quickly passed and suddenly them were getting ready to get off. With suitcases ready they slowly and quietly made their way down another gang plank and onto solid ground again.

Drucilla was the first down and as she stepped away from the gang plank she put her case down and did a little dance, she was so excited to be in another country. The others followed one by one with Harold bringing up the rear, although he had not been here for some time he had been here before so he was used to it. They made their way through the streets to where they were going to stay. It had taken half a day to get there and it would take half a day to get back, and they were determined to make the most of the three days in between.

Having reached the boarding house where they were staying they went to their rooms and unpacked their things, by now it was getting late so they decided to have something to eat next door in the cafe. Whilst they ate plans were made for the following day.

Finally, tired but happy they all said good night and went to bed.

The next three days were spent exploring the town, sitting on the top of the hill overlooking the harbour where they could watch the boats coming in and going out. Visiting the ruins of the old castle that was once the home of the regions rulers. The local market where they saw fish of all shapes, sizes and colour, crabs, shrimps and other things that had been caught by the fishing boats that they had seen in the harbour. They visited several cafes' where they ate many different things that they would not have eaten at home. They even managed to spend some time on the beach. Every night they returned to the boarding house they were very tired and slept soundly but they always looked forward to the next day.

Those three days past very quickly and it was soon time for them to pack everything back into the suitcases, say goodbye to the landlady and make their way to the harbour. As they approached the ferry they noticed that it was not the one that came out on, that meant that they could spend the next three hours exploring again. The journey seemed to flash by and before they knew it they were back on the bus back to Poundly Pond. It was four o'clock when they arrived outside Charlene's front gate, she said goodbye to her friends, hugged Harold and thanked him for organising the trip. As her front door shut the others were walking slowly down the road towards the centre of the village were Ricky would go one way, Harold and Drucilla the other. At the junction they too said goodbye and promised that they would do it again, only next time they would go somewhere different.

Eventually Harold and Drucilla reached their front gates that were next to each other, they said goodbye and slowly walked up to their front doors. Once inside they were both so tired that they went straight to bed where they slept soundly.

They had a wonderful time but they were all very glad to be back in their own homes and in their own beds.

THE POUNDLY POND FIREWORKS NIGHT

It was 5pm on this Thursday late in the afternoon and all the children from Poundly Pond and their friends from all the surrounding villages were getting quite excited as they gathered around an area that was roped off for safety, after all it was November 5th and they were all waiting for the fireworks display. At one end of the roped off area was where the bonfire was beginning to get bigger and provide some warmth around it so a few more were standing as close as the rope would let them.

Several of the parents were putting cakes, sausage rolls and crisps out on a table for the children, whilst others were getting the area ready to launch the fireworks.

It was getting closer and closer to 6pm which was when the fireworks display was going to start. Harold and Ricky carried two boxes out and each one had lids on to be safe, they now had all of the fireworks out and ready to pin some to a post which was one of the two that they were using. They also put some special fireworks in a different container near to a small table so that the change would be quicker.

Suddenly a fountain shape firework started to throw sparkles into the air because the display had started.

Next three rockets shot up into the sky and exploded into lots of twinkles as they lit up the area.

The large Catherine wheel started spinning around whilst another fountain shape firework was throwing sparkles up in the air but these sparkles then went bang one after the other, sometimes there were two bangs at the same time.

Next were another three rockets flying up into the sky and then they exploded all throwing out different colours.

Most of the children could be heard going ooh and arr, especially when the rockets exploded. A few more fountain and tubular displays on the little table were creating lots of noise, sparkles and coloured smoke. As they started dying down there were three small Catherine wheels spinning on the post.

They were followed by several tall round fireworks on the little table throwing up sparkles and small shoots, some went bang and some threw out more coloured smoke, these took a bit longer as they were much bigger. More oohs and arrs were still being heard.

Whilst this was going on nobody had noticed Harold and Ricky had been putting hollow poles into the ground into which they were putting quite a few more rockets. As the tall fireworks finally died down and all the children thought that was the end of the display, the first salvo of rockets that had been lit by Harold flew up into the sky, there were about ten of them going in all directions and lighting up the whole area except where the glow of the bonfire was gradually getting smaller. Suddenly a very big rocket shot into the sky and as it went bang there were lots of other bangs when sparkles seemed to be covering the area.

This was the last of the fireworks and everyone, including the children, clapped their hands to show how much they enjoyed the show. During the show some of the children were eating the cakes and sausage rolls whilst others were nibbling the crisps so most of the food had been eaten too.

Harold and Ricky started taking down the tables, the posts and collecting the rocket launchers whilst Drucilla and other parents were picking up just a few pieces of sweet wrappers that had been accidently dropped. George the Giraffe reached up to take the few rockets out of the trees that had fallen there.

Charlene was rolling up the rope that had been round the firework area but she left the one around the bonfire for safety. Then gradually the children went home to their beds whilst many of the parents went home for a rest.

It took a while for the children to calm down as they really enjoyed this years' firework display. Eventually Poundly pond was quiet again.

THE TREASURE HUNT

Time had passed so quickly at Poundly Pond since the sparkly and exciting firework display. Christmas had come and gone, all the decorations and lights had made the village look very festive and bright especially with the tree that was near to the middle of what was normally the sports area. Everyone was very happy because although it had been cold, it was dry except for a light covering of snow and everyone just put on jumpers and furry coats to make sure that they kept warm. The tree was also covered in lights, but it had quite a number of presents around it too for the children.

After a few days Harold, Ricky and Charlene started taking all the tree decorations down. Because he could reach much higher George the Giraffe took the decorations down that the others could not reach, even if two children helped whilst standing on Harold's and Ricky's shoulders.

Today was the next special time in Poundly Pond. It was Easter Time when many of the Rabbits and even a couple of the younger Hares were hopping around being the Easter Bunnies, some were even carrying Easter eggs to give to the children many of whom had also come out to run around, a few of the children from the surrounding villages had come to join in.

By then it was almost 12 o'clock when Drucilla was seen flying around swooping above the groups of 'Easter Bunnies' and children who had all been enjoying their chocolate. However, Drucilla was announcing that it was time for the annual Easter Treasure Hunt so gradually everyone collected together outside Harold's house to learn their tasks for the search. Firstly, they were told to be careful, not to climb the trees too high and there was nothing in the water, then they were told that there were a few items that were wrapped up in bright coloured wrapping paper, some were even in shiny paper. There were a few in boxes so they would have to be uncovered. Some were also quite high as they had been put in their place by Eric the Eagle, these were for those who could fly. At that point Mr Bruin, as he was the Mayor, said GO! And they all ran off in different directions whilst looking up into the trees and some were looking along the ground. A few of them stayed in pairs but most searched individually around the field in amongst the trees in the reasonable size forest that was between two of the villages.

As they searched a few squeals of delight, surprise and happiness could be heard as the treasures were being found and added to the scoreboard that enabled the treasures that had been found to be monitored, gradually the scoreboard was filling up.

Although a couple of the 'treasures' were cans of drink and a few of the boxes had cakes or biscuits in, some of the parents had prepared a few other things that everyone could eat, at different times some of those searching came back to where they started from for a drink or a piece of cake, there was even a kettle so hot drinks of tea and coffee could be made, some fruit juice that could be poured for those who wanted it, and obviously some biscuits and cakes. All these things were outside Harold's house on a table being organised by Mrs Bruin the Bear and Georgina the goose, even Sydney the Stork helped if there was a short queue.

Occasionally those who could fly were seen carrying small bright parcels that they had found. Louise the Monkey and Marie her sister had joined in too, they had found a box and were drinking from the caned drink that was inside, whilst Marie was walking and drinking she almost walked into Richard and Duchess but she just missed them as Louise called to her. The afternoon had gone quickly whilst they were having fun and the time had gone so quickly that it was almost 4 o'clock. Some of the children were gradually getting tired so were coming back to the table to finish the snacks and look at the scoreboard. A few of the children drifted back to their homes, some had a little to eat for tea and some just went to sleep in their warm beds. Even some of the parents were glad to be able to sit down and rest.

The scoreboard was full showing that everything had been found, these included a few cans of fizzy drinks. Some with chocolate cakes, others with biscuits in and there were a number of different toys. That was good as no one would have to remember where the treasures had been put and then recover them.

It had been an exciting day with all the children having found something so everyone was happy.

THE STORM

George, Leo and Eric had all been visiting Harold where they had been playing all sorts of games but after a good afternoon and evening it was getting late so they decided that it was time to go home. They all put on their hats and coats because it was still raining. It had been raining when they got up, it had been raining all morning, it had been raining when they came to Harold's and now it was still raining. Everywhere was so wet that there were puddles where there had never been puddles before. They wondered when it would stop, but they still had to go home so Harold opened the door and they all said goodbye. As George, Leo and Eric went home they noticed that the Pond had risen very high, so high in fact that in one place it was over the bank and spreading out over the grass. No one else was out in this horrible weather and they were not going to stay out any longer than they had to, so they went as quickly as they could. As each one reached their home they went inside, took off their coats and shook off the water and then shut the door.

As the darkness engulfed the village everyone was wrapped up snuggly in the comfort of their homes whilst outside it rained and rained. They all hoped that it would stop by the morning.

After his friends had gone Harold settled down to read a book, he sat on his settee with a cushion behind his head, a nice hot cup of chocolate on the table and a glowing fire in the grate. After a while, having drunk his chocolate and stoked up the fire Harold was deeply engrossed in the story. He was just about to enter the castle when there was an enormous crash outside that woke him from the story, next the whole room was lit up by a bright white light. Harold sat up so quickly that he knocked the little table over, it was a good job that he had finished the chocolate otherwise he would have spilt it all over the floor. Then there was another enormous crash followed immediately by another bright white flash of light that filled the room even through the closed curtains. Oh dear, thought Harold, I had hoped that the rain would stop but it seems to be getting worse.

Just as Harold reached the window to look outside there was yet another crash and flash of light only this time he saw that the flash of light was one of the biggest forks of lightning that he had ever seen, it went from one side of the sky to the other and lit up everything as far as his eyes could see. If this wasn't bad enough the wind had started to blow and all the trees were losing their leaves. Yes, he thought, Autumn is really here. He was already looking forward to next spring.

Closing the curtains Harold decided that it was time he went to bed although he would still read his book for a while. Harold went upstairs, cleaned his teeth, put on his pyjamas and curled up in his big bed, but he could hear the wind noise rising outside and the regular loud crash was followed by the bright white flash. He was glad that he was in the warm and hoped that his home would not be damaged. As Harold drifted off to sleep he also hoped that all of the village would be safe.

As most of the village slept the storm raged above them all night, the wind howled and tore at the flowers and trees, it even lifted a few tiles off the roof of the school, but because it was so dark between the flashes it was difficult to see what else was happening. The whole village would have to wait until morning.

Gradually the wind stopped blowing and the rain stopped falling. The dark black clouds gave way to a grey sky that was beginning to reflect the early light of the new day. Meanwhile the people in the village that had managed to stay asleep were beginning to wake. Some of them could not see very much as they looked out of their windows because they were away from the centre of the village and they could only see their front gardens. Others could see a few trees that had been blown down and flowers that had been flattened by the rain. But of those who lived near the centre of the village, the lucky ones could go out of their front doors, those who were not so lucky had to put on their wellingtons and paddle down their paths and along the road because the pond had grown. Half the village was covered with water, it surrounded the school and the village hall. The Church was built on slightly higher ground so it could be approached from one side, Mrs. Bruin's shop on the other side of the centre was dry, but the fields around the pond were completely covered. As the villagers came out to see what damage had been done they could see that many trees had been blown down, branches had been torn off others, some fences had disappeared others were drooping sadly. But as everyone gathered outside the Church it was discovered that none of the houses had been damaged at all. Although many of the houses had been surrounded by water none of them actually had water inside, they were all very lucky.

The people whose houses were high and dry helped those who were surrounded to try and brush some of the water away. Unfortunately, because the middle of the village was lower than the surrounding countryside they could not do anything about it. They had to wait for it to go into the ground or be dried up by the sun.

Harold went to make sure that Drucilla's house was still dry but as he tried to go out of her back door he found it was stuck and he could not move it at all. They went round the side of the house and discovered that the tree that had been growing beyond one corner of the house had been blown down and was right across the doorway. Drucilla had been very, very lucky. Whilst Harold cleared many of the small branches away Drucilla went to get some help because the tree was too big even for Harold. After about twenty minutes, Drucilla returned with Ricky and Robert. Sure enough with this strong help, they managed to pull the tree away from the door. They would have to cut the tree up later. Drucilla was sad that the tree had been blown down because it was very pretty in the spring with its beautiful pink blossom.
The next two days was spent trying to tidy up all the mess around the village. But although the water was draining away it was very slow and they could still not see half of the fields let alone the original pond. It took nearly two weeks before the outline of the

pond could be seen clearly again. Slowly the village returned to normal, the school roof was repaired, the fences put up again or renewed and most of the trees cut up for firewood. Everyone had a fire in their home so the wood would not be wasted.

A week after the storm Drucilla had been out for a walk in the woods where she and Harold had their treasure hunt. She had her wellingtons on because the ground was still very wet, and as she squelched along she was counting the number of trees that had been blown down ' 17, 18, 19, 20, 21"Oh' she said out loud 'this is so sad' she could see so many trees that had been blown down and promptly stopped counting because she did not want to depress herself any more. The pond here was still flooded but she could see the line where the water had reached so the water was going down.

As Drucilla slowly walked back home she wondered what the other ponds were like. She realised that Poundly Pond would never be the same after the storm, it had blown down so many lovely trees and torn branches off many more. But she was thankful that no one was hurt and nobody's house was damaged, although several had very near misses.

The following spring the village did not look quite as bright and cheerful as it used to with so many trees missing but there was nothing that anyone could do. That storm would be remembered for many years to come.

CHRISTMAS AT POUNDLY POND

As the weather finally became colder and winter gradually crept in, after all it was already past the middle of November. Some of the residents of Poundly Pond had started to wear warmer clothing after the Autumn that had been much warmer than it usually was. Even most of the growth around the pond had become almost sad as at least half of it had died off getting ready for next year.

Then one morning as everyone started their day they looked out of their window to see that suddenly everywhere had a slight covering of snow that had fallen overnight. Now it could be seen that it really was winter, and even Poundly Pond had a very thin covering of ice around the edges. As December started to move forward

and a little more snow had been falling on several nights and even on a couple of days, some of the younger ones had been playing snowballs. A couple of sledges had been taken out of storage and were being pulled around. Even some of the older ones in Poundly Pond were starting to get their decorations out of storage too as the thoughts of how they were going to be arranged this year.
By the middle of December several decorations had been put up, after al it was only 10 days to go all of the houses had decorations in their windows and over the next few days most of the houses had decorations around their roofs, it was looking very pretty and the snow made it look even better.

Harold had some help putting his decorations right up to the top of the roof and there were even bells at each corner. There were a couple of houses that had lights looped along and around their roofs. On the 17th December a big sledge arrived in Poundly Pond being pulled by four horses carrying the traditional Christmas Fir Tree. Several of the residents had dug quite a big hole to put it in, then they filled it in and made sure that it would not fall down. Harold had even walked on the soil. To make sure that would not happen there had even been three rope supports.

For most of that last week leading up to Christmas Day more decorations had been put up around and on the rest of the houses. The central tree was decorated right to the top, it was so tall that a few of the birds had helped Drucilla reach the top with the lights. A few of the closer big trees even had decorations strung between them, they even went to the main tree.

This year there were some new special decorative lights that made it easier for everyone to see their way to their front doors, especially with the snow on the ground. There were quite a few solar-powered LED lights that were on both sides of the paths making the whole area look very pretty and decorative.

The younger ones still continued to play in the snow, so in some places it was quite trodden down even sleigh tracks seem to be everywhere.

Finally, as the 23rd December came to an end the excitement of Christmas Eve the next day had nearly reached its climax as several of those from the other local villages started getting together to sing a few Special Christmas songs. Most of those in Poundly Pond all joined in and sung these songs: -

Can you sing some too?

1) We Wish You a Merry Christmas
2) Rudolf the Red Nose Reindeer
3) Jingle Bells
4) 12 days of Christmas
5) Santa Claus is Coming to Town

Finally, everyone went round and on their way some were still singing as they walked home
and eventually they went to bed quite tired where they slept until the special day. In many
houses the food was being prepared for Christmas Day so that

everyone could enjoy it. .
On Christmas Day morning many of the younger ones woke up a little early, and on looking
out of the window discovered that even more snow had fallen overnight and covered all the
younger ones play marks. Even the main tree had areas that had been covered up.

They all had their breakfast and started to open their presents. A few of those who did not
 have any younger ones went out slipping and sliding through the snow to give their friends
their presents.
Meanwhile although a few others went out in the snow, most stayed inside and waited for
their special Christmas Lunch.
After they finished eating several went back outside to play in the snow and enjoy
themselves.

NOTE: (This could be printed at the end of this story or at the beginning to help the reader remember the lyrics).

A Few Top Children's Christmas Songs
Christmas is one of the most celebrated holidays in the world. It represents love, friendship,
compassion, and the act of giving to others. Music is a big part of the holiday and it tends to

bring out the Christmas spirit in everyone. Some of those songs are here.

Rudolf the Red Nosed Reindeer

Rudolph, the red-nosed reindeer had a very shiny nose.
And if you ever saw it you would even say it glows.
All of the other reindeer used to laugh and call him names.
They never let poor Rudolph join in any reindeer games.
Then one foggy Christmas eve Santa came to say
Rudolph, with your nose so bright, won't you guide my sleigh tonight?

Jingle Bells

Dashing through the snow, in a one-horse open sleigh
Over the fields we go, laughing all the way
Bells on bob-tails ring, making spirits bright
What fun it is to laugh and sing a sleighing song tonight.
Jingle bells, jingle bells, jingle all the way
Oh what fun it is to ride in a one-horse open sleigh
Jingle bells, jingle bells, jingle all the way
Oh what fun it is to ride in a one-horse open sleigh.
Santa Claus is Coming to Town
You'd better watch out, you better not cry
You'd better not pout, I'm telling you why
Santa Claus is coming to town
He's making a list and checking it twice

He's gonna find out who's naughty and nice
Santa Claus is coming to town
He sees you when you're sleeping
He knows when you're awake
He knows if you've been bad or good
So be good for goodness sake
Oh, you'd better watch out, you better not cry
Better not pout, I'm telling you why
Santa Claus is coming to town.

We Wish You a Merry Christmas
We wish you a merry Christmas
And a happy New Year
Good tidings we bring to you and your kin
Good tidings for Christmas and a happy New Year

Copyright @2022 by David Underhill

All rights reserved. No part of this book may be reproduced in any form or by any electronic or mechanical means, including information storage and retrieval systems, without permission in writing from the publisher, except by reviewers, who may quote brief passages in a review.

This publication contains the opinions and ideas of It's author. It is intended to provide helpful and informative material on the subjects addressed in the publication. The author and publisher specifically disclaim all responsibility for any liability, loss or risk, personal or otherwise, which is incurred as a consequence, directly or indirectly, of the use and application of any of the contents of this book.

WORKBOOK PRESS LLC
187 E Warm Springs Rd,
Suite B285, Las Vegas, NV 89119, USA

Website: https://workbookpress.com/
Hotline: 1-888-818-4856
Email: admin@workbookpress.com

Ordering Information:
Quantity sales. Special discounts are available on quantity purchases by corporations, associations, and others.
For details, contact the publisher at the address above.

Library of Congress Control Number:

ISBN-13:   978-1-960752-92-5 (Paperback Version)
           978-1-960752-93-2 (Digital Version)

REV. DATE: 09/08/2022

ABOUT THE AUTHOR

It is nice to be able to say hello to all my new friends and to thank you for reading my new book, I hope you enjoy the stories because there will be some more. I have been writing different stories for about 10 years but I never believed that I would ever have them published, so this is really a lifetimes dream come true. The idea for Poundly Pond was developed out of a very short story that was written by Samantha when she was at school and about 8 years old. Initially it just sat in a file until I found it and had the idea of creating a few of the characters, hence Harold and Drucilla. But they needed somewhere to live so, Poundly was conceived and whilst I was looking at the image in my head I could see the Pond near the middle of the village. So Poundly Pond could not be there with just two occupants and gradually the village and the stories grew around it.

So welcome to Poundly Pond and all those in and around it.

Well I am nearly 68 years young, I was born in London and now live in Poole, Dorset yet I still feel like I am only 40 (most of the time). I have been physically fortunate all my life and carried out a number of activities from climbing, sky diving, sailing dinghies, fortunately I can swim as they have dumped me in the water on numerous occasions, to racing Karts and even cars, plus water skiing and surfing. Obviously I used play football and cricket. There are still numerous activities on my list so who knows what comes next? Samantha and Jade assisted with ideas and a few Illustrations as the stories continued to develop. I look forward to bringing more stories about the inhabitants of Poundly Pond.